THIS CANDLEWICK BOOK BELONGS TO:

_____

_____

_____

For Pat
A. M.

For Jo and her family
and all the Jack Russells
they have loved
S. R.

First U.S. paperback edition 2019

Library of Congress Catalog Card Number 2016951634
ISBN 978-0-7636-8948-3 (hardcover)
ISBN 978-1-5362-0892-4 (paperback)

19 20 21 22 23 24 CCP 10 9 8 7 6 5 4 3 2 1

Printed in Shenzhen, Guangdong, China

This book was typeset in Clarendon T Light and Keswick.
The illustrations were done in mixed media.

Candlewick Press
99 Dover Street
Somerville, Massachusetts 02144

visit us at www.candlewick.com

Our Very Own DOG

Taking Care of Your First Pet

Amanda McCardie

illustrated by

Salvatore Rubbino

CANDLEWICK PRESS

A dog came to live with us
when I was four.

For a minute or two she sat next to me.
Then she climbed right over my back and nuzzled
my hand with her cold, wet nose.

Hello, Sophie!

Sophie had been living at an animal shelter.

Now she had her own home—with us.

We had prepared everything for our new dog:

a cozy bed and blankets,

bowls for food and water,

a toy to sleep with

and one to chew,

a ball, a leash,

and a collar.

A chew toy is useful because dogs need to chew.
It's natural, calming, and good for their teeth.

If a dog's collar fits properly, a grown-up should be able to slip two fingers under it.

We fit her collar and felt it with our fingers
to make sure it wasn't too tight.
It had a metal tag on it that
jingled as she walked.

There, Sophie!

A dog's tag should be engraved with the owner's address and telephone number.

A shy or nervous dog may feel threatened if you look too closely into her face.

Sophie was nervous around my father at first, so he was careful not to look into her eyes or pet her or get too close.

Instead, he spoke to her gently and made her the yummiest dinners.

Soon she came to love him best of all.

11

As a dog, Sophie couldn't talk, but she learned to understand a few commands.

"Sit."

"Stay."

"Come."

"Heel."

Training works best when it is kind, patient, and the same every time.

A dog who walks "to heel" won't rush into a busy road.

She also knew
her own name,

"Sophie!"

though she sometimes pretended not to.

A dog's whiskers
are useful "feelers."

And she always heard the words "Time for a walk,"
even if you whispered them.

Good dog owners
scoop poop!

Dogs should be let off the
leash only in places where
it's permitted and only
if they can be trusted to
come when they're called.

All dogs need regular exercise.

We took Sophie walking every day so she could run and roll, sniff smells, and meet other dogs.

There are more than 400 breeds of dogs. Many dogs are a mixture of breeds.

Dogs are highly sociable animals who want lots of company.

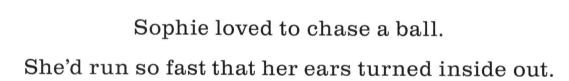

Sophie loved to chase a ball.

She'd run so fast that her ears turned inside out.

Go, Sophie!

She'd drop the ball
for you to throw—

then snatch it
up herself.

Dogs can't sweat to cool down the way we do (except on the pads of their paws).
Panting helps to cool them when they get hot.

Sophie could move quickly when she wanted to,
as we found out when she first
smelled sausages.

A dog's sense of smell is
one to ten thousand times
more sensitive than a person's.
Smells are important to dogs.

Hey, Sophie!

Those were for us!

Sophie enjoyed being scratched and petted—and loved it when we brushed her in those hard-to-reach places.

A dog should have her own brush and comb for grooming.

Most dogs like to be petted by their owners, but many don't want to be touched by strangers. Always ask the owner before you touch a dog.

But she didn't like being washed.

She liked it better when *we* had baths.

Shoo, Sophie!

Sophie never minded getting dirty.
One day, she splashed through every puddle
in the park, then shook out her fur to get dry.

Oh, Sophie!

Shaking is a highly efficient
way for a dog to get dry—
much quicker than a towel!

As we made our muddy way back home,

we passed a big sign that said DOG SHOW.

We only went to take a look.

We weren't even thinking about entering Sophie.

But Sophie wagged her
tail at the judge and
gazed up into his eyes.

Can you guess who
won the prize that day
for the friendliest dog?

It was Sophie!

Your Very Own Dog

If you are thinking about getting a dog, it's important to find out as much about dogs as you can and to figure out which kind of dog would best suit your family.

You can learn from books, dog owners, rescue centers, trainers, and vets, and by watching and listening to the dogs you meet. Every bark, whine, and whimper has a meaning. Dogs also "speak" with their bodies, eyes, ears, and tails. A dog whose language you understand will be your friend for life.

friendly

happy

playful

How-ow-owl!

lonely

frightened

A Few Useful Books About Dogs

Puppy Training for Kids by Colleen Pelar (Barron's, 2012), *The Dog Expert* by Karen Bush with Dr. D. G. Hessayon (Expert, 2010), and *Do Dogs Dream?* by Stanley Coren (Norton, 2012).

Index

Look up the pages to find out about all these doggy things. Don't forget to look at both kinds of words—**this kind** and *this kind*.

bathing . . . 21

breeds . . . 15

chewing . . . 8

collars . . . 8–9

diet . . . 11

grooming . . . 20

leashes . . . 8, 14

panting . . . 17

petting . . . 20

poop . . . 14

running . . . 15, 16

shaking . . . 22

smells . . . 15, 18

training . . . 11, 12

wagging . . . 24

walking . . . 14–15

whiskers . . . 13

Amanda McCardie is the author of several books for young readers, including *A Book of Feelings*. About this book, she says, "Sophie is dear to my heart. She was the cheery, cheeky little dog I grew up with in real life." Amanda McCardie lives in London.

Salvatore Rubbino is the award-winning illustrator of *Just Ducks!*, *A Walk in London*, *A Walk in New York*, *A Walk in Paris*, and *Harry Miller's Run*. About this book, he says, "I have always been fond of cats! But by studying dogs and watching their fascinating behavior, I now find that I love dogs, too!" Salvatore Rubbino lives in London.